365 ways to
Love your child

QUANTITY SALES

Most Dell books are available at special quantity discounts when purchased in bulk by corporations, organizations, or groups. Special imprints, messages, and excerpts can be produced to meet your needs. For more information, write to: Dell Publishing, 1540 Broadway, New York, NY 10036. Attention: Director, Special Markets.

INDIVIDUAL SALES

Are there any Dell books you want but cannot find in your local stores? If so, you can order them directly from us. You can get any Dell book currently in print. For a complete up-to-date listing of our books and information on how to order, write to: Dell Readers Service, Box DR, 1540 Broadway, New York, NY 10036.

365 Ways to Love Your Child

Alex J. Packer, Ph.D.

A Dell Trade Paperback

A DELL TRADE PAPERBACK
Published by
Dell Publishing
a division of
Bantam Doubleday Dell Publishing Group, Inc.
1540 Broadway
New York, New York 10036

The trademark Dell® is registered in the
U.S. Patent and Trademark Office.

Library of Congress Cataloging in Publication Data

Packer, Alex J., 1951–
    365 ways to love your child / Alex J. Packer.
        p   cm.
    ISBN 0-440-50590-9
    1. Parent and child.   2. Parenting.   I. Title.   II. Title: Three hundred sixty-five ways to love your child.
    HQ755.85.P33   1995
    649′.1—dc20   94-48755
                                                                                      CIP

Printed in the United States of America
Published simultaneously in Canada
September 1995
10 9 8 7 6 5 4 3 2 1
CWO

To Ned and Sue Hallowell
for their love, support, and superb dinners.

Acknowledgments

I am deeply grateful to the following parents and teenagers for the child-raising advice they so generously shared with me: Lyn Bliss, Jeff and Lynn Cebula, Pamela Espeland, Stephen Gustin, Kip Hale, Sue Hallowell, Esther Kattef, Jonah Klevesahl, Jack Peckham, Sherman Todd, and Jack and Suzanne Winter-Rose.

I would also like to thank my agent, Gail Ross, for her advice and support, and the Authors Guild for their tireless efforts on behalf of writers everywhere.

Finally, I would like to thank the many parents and children I have known who unknowingly contributed to this book by showing me how respectful, loving parent-child relationships are built.

365 Ways to Love Your Child

1. Play hooky with your child one day a year.

❂

2. If you want your child to talk to you, don't ridicule what he says.

❂

3. Tune your parental radar so that it scans for success, not failure.

✸

4. The next time your child questions your authority, remember, you're the one who told him to stand up for his principles.

✸

5. Knock before entering your child's room.

✸

6. Don't label your child a crybaby, liar, or selfish, spoiled brat. He might decide to live down to it.

7. When you feel yourself getting angry, count to ten. For really serious conflicts, count to 10,000. Then sleep on it.

8. Support a cause together. March. Petition. Share. Care.

9. If God had intended homes to be museums, he would have put children in glass cases.

10. Never criticize your child in public.

✹

11. Never criticize your child in private.

✹

12. Never criticize your child. If you must, criticize only her actions.

✹

13. When your children are least lovable is when they need you to love them the most.

✹

14. For every minute you spend telling your child about her faults, spend ten minutes telling her about her virtues.

✹

15. Let your child keep her room any way she likes—as long as she keeps the house any way you like.

16. Don't try to win arguments. Try to solve problems.

17. Spend time with each of your children separately.

✸

18. If you want your children to respect the value of money, discuss family finances with them.

✸

19. Have your teenager write the checks as one of her chores.

20. Never threaten your child. Chances are you won't follow through anyway.

21. If you are hesitant about extending a freedom, offer your child a "trial period" so he can prove his responsibility.

✿

22. Remember that most conflict between parents and children is not personal. It is generational.

✿

23. Listen more. Talk less.

✿

24. Recognize that many of the battles you have with your child exist because you create them in your mind. They stem from your tastes and preferences and have little to do with any objective definition of right and wrong.

25. Go camping.

26. Never say "I told you so." Your child knows you told him so.

27. Slip a surprise into your child's coat pocket.

28. Remember that your children are not you.

29. Don't lecture your child about honesty. Be honest.

30. Don't lecture your child about hard work. Work hard.

✹

31. Don't lecture your child about showing respect. Be respectful.

✹

32. Never compare your children to one another.

33. Tell your kids when you've had a rough day.

34. Compliment your child's friends.

35. The job of a parent is not to find a child's weaknesses, but to find a child's strengths.

36. Don't be impatient with your child's questions. He's just trying to discover the world.

✹

37. Every day, think of ten things about your child for which you are grateful.

✹

38. Let your kids plan the vacation.

✹

39. Whenever you think it's time to talk to your child about the facts of life, you're probably several years too late.

40. Never tell an embarrassing story about your child in his presence.

41. Or behind his back.

✿

42. Imagine how you would feel if somebody spoke to you the way you speak to your child. Let that be your guide.

✿

43. Be careful about blaming children for things they didn't do. Kids, too, are innocent until proven guilty.

✵

44. Prepare your child for tomorrow by focusing on the quality of today.

✵

45. Never laugh at your child's dreams.

46. Call your child from work.

47. Your time is dearer to your children than your money. Be lavish with the first and moderate with the second.

48. Remember that children are not servants.

49. If your child tells you something in confidence, keep it confidential.

50. Don't berate your child in front of her friends.

✹

51. Practice parenthood's most powerful phrases:

> "Nice try!"
> "Good job!"
> "Great catch!"
> "I'm so proud of you!"
> "You look nice!"
> "I know you can do it!"
> "I trust you."

52. Take each of your children on a dinner date once a month.

53. Send your child an "I Love You" telegram.

54. Don't punish your child. Instead, allow her to experience the consequences of her actions.

55. To tell whether a given response to your child's behavior is a punishment or a consequence, ask yourself:

• Does the response help my child to understand *why* what she did was wrong?

• Does it allow my child to assume responsibility for her behavior? To make amends? Undo damage? Soothe hurt feelings?

• Does it give my child a chance to show that she can be more responsible, sensitive, and trustworthy in the future?

56. Teach your children that failure is a friend that can bring them one step closer to success.

57. Admit when you are wrong. Nothing hurts a parent's credibility more than infallibility.

58. Let your children choose their own clothes.

59. Remember that it's not conflict that harms relation-ships. It's *unresolved* conflict that harms relationships.

60. Once a day, tell your child you love him. Do it twice on Sundays.

61. Hug your teenagers.

62. Respond to your child's disappointments with empathy, not judgment.

EMPATHY, YES!		JUDGMENT, NO!
It hurts to feel lonely.	vs.	How can you feel lonely? You have lots of friends.
I know how much making the team meant to you.	vs.	You'll get over it.
That must have been very embarrassing.	vs.	If you feel that way you're being silly.

63. Don't ask your child to make *you* proud. Ask him to make *himself* proud.

64. Mistakes are how children learn to make better choices the next time.

✸

65. Let your child know that you trust him to do the right thing.

✸

66. The way to get your child to change is to love him just the way he is.

✸

67. Never say: "Don't you dare get angry with me." Instead, say: "You can be angry with me, but you can't (hit, talk like that, etc.)."

68. Remember that rules are there to serve. Not to rule.

69. When your child is "going through a stage," whatever you do, don't tell him.

✸

70. Give yourself a quiz: What are your child's fears, dreams, current projects, favorite activities/books/movies/school subjects? Who are your child's friends, heroes, and teachers? If you can't answer questions such as these, you need to get more involved in your child's world.

71. Good parenting, like democracy, is messy and cumbersome. (Only tyranny is efficient.)

72. Make your child the hero of his bedtime stories.

73. Remember: The purpose of discipline is to teach, not punish.

74. Don't try to give your kids all the right answers. Try to ask the right questions.

75. Be there when your kids need you. Get out of the way when they don't.

76. The next time you nag your child to do something, remember that words repeated over and over eventually lose their meaning.

77. If you focus on the quality of what's *inside* the home, you won't have to worry about the quality of what's *outside* the home.

78. Don't snoop.

79. Remember that the things most parents worry about usually don't happen.

80. Appoint your children to be "family health monitors." Put each child in charge of a different aspect of family health: recreation, stress reduction, nutrition, etc.

81. Let your children know that your interest in their where-abouts is a sign of caring, not mistrust.

82. A parent's greatest tool is the power of example.

83. The second greatest tool is a sense of humor.

84. The worth of a child is not measured by a report card.

85. Raising children is the ongoing process of letting go.

✺

86. Next time you're tempted to tell your child what *you* think, ask her to tell you what *she* thinks.

✺

87. Try to look at conflicts from the vantage point of someone who is not under the sway of love and pride of ownership. Ask yourself: How would I react if this were one of my child's friends instead of my child?

88. Don't try to talk your child out of her feelings.

89. Model values that encourage self-discipline and high moral standards and you needn't fear letting your child make her own decisions.

90. Remember that children want to be good. They want to succeed, they want to be thought well of, and they want to think well of themselves.

✵

91. "Sticks and stones may break my bones but names will never hurt me." This is a crock. When parents sling verbal stones, children get hurt.

✵

92. Keep in mind that a child's school problems sometimes indicate strengths: creativity, curiosity, a well-developed sense of justice.

93. Help your child to build an extended community for herself.

94. Remind your kids that most mistakes can be undone, repaired, forgotten, or apologized for.

95. Treat your child the way you would like her to treat others.

96. Remember that it is acceptance, not praise, that builds self-esteem. Praise just builds a dependency on the opinions of others for one's sense of self-worth.

97. Let go of battles whose sole purpose is to establish the supremacy of your opinion.

98. Being right doesn't solve the problem.

✹

99. You cannot control your child. All you can do is create an environment that encourages him to control himself. This environment can be created out of guilt, fear, and abuse, or out of love, reason, and example.

✹

100. To change a catastrophe into a challenge, change your attitude.

✺

101. Avoid making assumptions before you know the facts.

✺

102. Trust in your child's ability to solve most problems by himself.

103. The next time your child annoys you, remember that he acts that way, not to annoy you, but because he's a child.

104. Don't give advice unless asked.

105. Meditate.

✷

106. Let your child know that you're always available to talk.

✷

107. If all you see is what's wrong with your kids, in time, that is all that they will see.

✻

108. Explain the reasoning behind rules. You want your child to see that the rule exists, not because somebody said so, but because the idea contained in it makes sense.

✻

109. Remember that it is only by having the opportunity to exercise judgment that children learn good judgment.

110. If you leave the house before your child is awake or come home after she goes to bed, place a note or drawing on her pillow.

111. Punishment, instead of suppressing misbehavior, often just drives it underground. It teaches children, not right and wrong, but how to become craftier at avoiding detection.

✹

112. Never spank. Never slap. (There's a word for people who take advantage of their size to pick on little kids: bullies.)

✹

113. Learn the names of your child's friends.

✹

114. It is never humility that undermines authority. It is the pretense of perfection.

115. Earn your child's respect. If respect is demanded, it is not respect children feel, but fear.

116. Don't measure the quality of your family relationships by how much conflict you have. Measure it by how effectively and lovingly you solve that conflict.

✵

117. The next time you say to your child—"Because I have more experience, that's why!"—remember that experience can blind as well as enlighten.

✵

118. Be silly.

✵

119. It is in the nature of children to run through interests as quickly as they do sneakers. Don't think of this as a lack of perseverance. Think of it as an excess of enthusiasm.

120. Remember that learning to walk is the process of "failing" one's way to mastery.

※

121. If you constantly remind your children of their past errors and future expectations, what kind of a "present" is that?

※

122. The next time you're at loggerheads with your child, ask yourself:

- What assumptions am I making that I'm not aware of?

- What "shoulds" and "musts" have I accepted without question?

- What is the basis for the limits I have imposed?

123. When parents become more accepting, it's amazing how their children become more acceptable.

124. Never forget that the condition of a child's room is insignificant when compared to the condition of his character.

125. A parent should be a representative of reality, not an agent of punishment.

✸

126. Establish a "command central" communications post for your family—a place where you can pin up messages, schedules, reminders, lists of chores, extra jobs for pay, family goals, funny cartoons, interesting articles, etc.

✸

127. Keep in mind that being neat isn't the same as being responsible.

128. Don't enable disorganization by covering up for your child's mistakes. Allow *her* to smooth ruffled feathers, pay library fines, reschedule missed appointments.

129. Think of disagreements as problems to be solved rather than personalities to be changed.

✷

130. If you must push your child, push her toward play and joy, passion and open-mindedness.

131. Children learn to love by receiving it.

✸

132. Since "bad behavior" is insensitivity to the needs, rights, and feelings of others, respond to your child's wrongdoings by focusing on the effects of her actions. This builds empathy, which is the foundation of prosocial behavior.

✸

133. Don't tease your child about her appearance or body.

134. Respond as a family to those in need.

135. Don't preach. Explain.

136. Attribute good intentions to your child.

137. Avoid statements that proclaim rightness. Instead of saying: "You're doing it wrong," say: "Let me show you how I learned to do it."

✹

138. Invite your child's friends along on family outings.

✹

139. Provide opportunities for your children to do good deeds. Encourage them to bake a pie for the new family down the street, or to rake the leaves for an elderly neighbor.

✹

140. At the earliest age, involve your child in tasks mean-
ingful to the family's functioning (sorting laundry, setting the table, pumping gas, etc.).

✹

141. Remember that you cannot change your child. All you
can do is change your own behavior toward your
child.

142. Ask your child to help you with something very important.

143. Try to see things, and hear things, from your child's perspective.

144. Don't give your child material rewards for good behavior. Such rewards undermine the intrinsic satisfaction derived from helping others.

145. Take your kids to visit an airport control tower.

146. Agree to disagree.

147. Look for progress, not perfection.

148. "You're acting like a child" is never an insult.

＊

149. Keeping the truth from children does not protect them. It causes them to doubt their perceptions.

＊

150. Give your child a generous gift: the pleasure of earning something.

151. It is through exposure to bacteria that a child builds up his immune system. Don't shield your child from the harsher realities of life. It won't protect him; it will only prevent him from learning to protect himself.

152. Read to your child.

153. Don't use "quality time" as an excuse for how little time you spend with your children. Quantity counts, too.

154. Teach your children that feelings are not right or wrong, good or bad. They just are. It's what you do with the feelings that counts.

✵

155. If your child pushes for more independence, take it as a sign that you are doing your job well.

✵

156. Let your kids daydream. Otherwise they'll never get anywhere in life.

157. When you are irritable, be alert to the possibility that it stems from the natural resentment parents can feel in response to their child's youth, options, and energy.

158. Don't focus on all the little things that need fixing. Focus on all the big things that don't.

159. When you say hurtful things to your child, you not only hurt her, you teach her how to be hurtful.

160. It is better to provide children with encouragement than evaluation.

161. Remember that each day you have with your child will never be repeated.

162. Treat your child's emotional wounds as you would his physical ones. Allow him his pain, do what you can to alleviate it, and then trust in his ability to heal himself.

☀

163. Don't respond to behavior in terms of gender stereotypes: "Boys shouldn't cry"; "That isn't ladylike."

☀

164. Take conflict to a private setting. It's hard enough without having an audience.

165. It's not what you say, it's how you say it.

166. Before you criticize, condemn, or punish, consider if there is a kinder, more effective way to make your point.

✹

167. If you tell your child to think before she acts, be sure you show her how.

✹

168. Sometimes the best thing you can do for your child is nothing.

169. Rules don't prevent bad behavior. Self-control does.

170. Visualize positive things for your child.

171. Don't forget that the only power your children have to control your mood is that which you give them.

172. A child is not a possession.

173. The traits that bother us most about our children are usually those found within ourselves.

174. Do not fear your child's anger. It is an expression of his trust in the steadfastness of your love. When you stand firm in the face of your child's anger you reciprocate that trust.

175. Try to remember what *your* parents did that you vowed you would never do to your own children.

176. A child's wish to spend time alone is not a rejection of you but an acceptance of himself.

�֍

177. Take heart that many of your child's most annoying traits—stubbornness, impulsivity, starry-eyedness—are those which, when tempered by maturity, will be most valuable to him.

✖

178. Be a model—not a molder.

179. When your child asks you for advice, advise her to do what she thinks is right. Then help her to figure out what that is.

180. Children should not have to compete at home.

✻

181. Don't yell. Your child won't be able to hear what you're saying.

✻

182. When your child must go along with rigid definitions of "rightness," support her perspective if she questions them. This makes it easier for her to accept arbitrary or unfair authority because it validates her take on reality.

183. Believe in your child's fundamental goodness. There is as much of it as you are willing to find.

✸

184. Lighten up.

✸

185. Build a bonfire.

✸

186. Don't ask your child to keep secrets from your spouse.

187. Trust your child. Even when you are not sure. If your trust is misplaced, your child will feel guilty. If it is well placed, your child will feel secure. Either outcome promotes growth.

188. When you confront your child with a wrongdoing, don't accuse—describe.

ACCUSATION, NO!		DESCRIPTION, YES!
"Do you think you can just ignore me when I ask you to do something?"	vs.	"I see that your room hasn't been cleaned up yet."
"You're so careless!"	vs.	"I'm angry that my tools were left out in the rain."
"How could you be so stupid?"	vs.	"Leaving your coat on the bus was a forgetful thing to do."

189. Go to every one of your child's games, concerts, and plays that you possibly can.

190. If you tell your child he'll never amount to anything if he doesn't buckle down, you're telling him he doesn't amount to anything now.

191. Sleep under the stars.

✷

192. Think of one problem you and your child have that you can solve today.

✷

193. Remember that the purpose of children is to teach adults patience.

✻

194. The word "patience" comes from the Latin word for suffering.

✻

195. If you want your children's cooperation, let them participate in the decision-making process.

✻

196. Kiss your children good night.

✷

197. Make a list of all your strengths as a parent.

✷

198. When in doubt about what to say to your child, tell her the truth about what you are feeling.

❄

199. Next time you have a conflict with your child, present it as a brain teaser you have to solve together.

❄

200. Ask for help.

❄

201. Choose your battles carefully.

✹

202. Keep in mind that much of your child's behavior bothers you, not because it is inherently wrong or immoral, but because you experience it as an adult (**n.** a grown-up variety of the human species identifiable by the inordinate emphasis it places on cleanliness, neatness, and obedience).

✹

203. If you can define a problem, you're halfway to the solution.

✿

204. Tell lots of jokes.

✿

205. Don't forget that it's usually the best parents who feel insecure and wonder if what they're doing is right.

✸

206. The most powerful motivator of self-control is not fear, guilt, or intellect. It is empathy.

✸

207. The most difficult task a child needs to learn is the one most rarely taught: how to experience and handle emotions.

☀

208. Good relationships with children, like all relation-ships, don't just happen. You have to work at them.

☀

209. Bury a family time capsule.

☀

210. Think of one thing you don't have to do today that would free up some time to be with your child.

✸

211. Take a course in CPR together.

✸

212. Honor your commitments. It's how children learn responsibility.

✸

213. Don't discount your child's opinion just because she's a child. Sometimes kids have the best ideas precisely *because* they are children.

✸

214. Keep in mind that most of the things you "can't stand" about your child you already are standing.

215. Invite interesting people over to the house. Allow your kids to socialize with them in age-appropriate ways.

216. Don't decide how you're going to answer before you hear the question.

217. If you and your children lead busy lives, make appointments to see one another.

218. Read parenting books. Learn what's appropriate at different stages in your child's development.

219. Child abuse occurs when parental expectations collide with behavior the child cannot change.

220. Don't take the "terrible twos" personally. They reflect your child's growing independence and initiative.

221. It is more important to let children know the privileges for good behavior than the punishments for bad.

222. Do talk to your kids about "when you were their age." Just don't do it in the middle of a lecture.

223. Schedule regular "family checkups"—once-a-week meetings when the whole family gathers to plan, to talk, and to solve problems.

224. Don't play favorites.

225. Have theme dinners.

226. Remember that parents who are perfectionists can never be satisfied with their children.

227. Ask your child what she would do if she had a magic wand.

✸

228. Take risks.

✸

229. Toast marshmallows.

230. Play. It's one of the great fringe benefits of having kids.

231. When your child doesn't want your help, don't feel rejected. Feel successful.

232. Many of your child's faults can be eliminated quite easily by a change in attitude—yours.

233. Look on the bright side. Think of your child as:

principled	rather than	stubborn
spontaneous	rather than	impulsive
passionate	rather than	overemotional

234. One of the most selfish things a parent can do is to unfailingly sacrifice her own needs to those of her children.

235. Never take your child's successes for granted. It diminishes his efforts.

236. Don't hurry Mother Nature. She has put a lot of thought into determining the rate at which children grow best.

237. Try not to react to your child's outer behavior. Use it as a clue to understanding what's going on inside your child. React to *that*.

238. Give your children lots of practice at receiving compliments.

239. Next time you say—"You kids are driving me crazy!" —ask yourself if you really want them to think they have that much power.

✹

240. Find something your child can teach you.

241. To gain perspective in the middle of a conflict, ask yourself: "How important would this be if my child suddenly began to have convulsions?"

242. Don't be fooled by those "perfect" parents you see. They lose their tempers, too, when no one's watching.

243. At the beginning of every day, picture the type of relationship you would like to have with your child.

244. Don't think of conflict as a challenge to your authority. Think of it as a challenge to your creativity.

�֎

245. React to your child's efforts to become responsible and trustworthy as you would to her efforts to speak—with patience, joy, encouragement, humor, gentle correction, and a fine example.

✖

246. Don't gush unless you really mean it. False praise cheapens all praise.

247. The best thing you can do when you don't know how to respond to your child's behavior is to ask: "What do *you* think we should do?"

248. Do not use the past as a weapon.

✸

249. Replace your fears with faith. You'll find there's much less to worry about.

✸

250. Don't project the rest of your child's life onto today's events.

✹

251. When self-pity tempts you to ask—"What have I done to deserve a child with all these faults?"—to be fair, you must also ask—"What have I done to deserve a child with all these virtues?"

✹

252. Clip articles that you think will interest a particular child and then discuss them with her.

❄

253. When your child says, "I'm sorry," ask her to tell you what she's sorry for. This helps her to link her behavior to the damage or hurt it caused.

❄

254. If the best answer you can give your child is "Because I said so!" perhaps she was right to ask "Why?"

✸

255. Base limits on morality, safety, courtesy, practicality, and your child's demonstrated level of responsibility —not on whim, "shoulds," or what others do.

✸

256. Take good care of your children by taking good care of yourself.

✹

257. Don't brag about your child to anyone—except grandparents. It embarrasses your child and makes everyone else dislike him.

✹

258. Next time you're feeling impatient about your child's rate of development, consider how miraculous it is that children are able to master so much so quickly.

✻

259. When you go to one of your child's games, cheer *all* the kids.

✻

260. Don't smoke.

✻

261. Tell your children that they do not always have to "try their hardest" and "do their best." There are times when "just showing up" and "doing as much as you have to" are more than enough.

✻

262. Before you chastise your child, consider that he may have already identified and learned from his mistake.

✻

263. Remember that your feelings about your child are not caused by what he does, but by what you *think* about what he does.

264. Always have a family goal.

265. Grant your children the right to hold childish thoughts.

266. And to disagree with their parents.

267. Instead of yelling, "Don't touch!" place valuable objects out of your child's reach.

268. Instead of scolding your child for tearing his clothes, give him old clothes to play in. (See 331.)

269. When you feel overwhelmed by things to "fix" in your child, make a list of them. Then ask yourself:

• Which are none of my business?

• Which are beyond my power or right to control?

• Which aren't going to matter a week from now?

Now deal with the one item that's left.

✹

270. Remember that being honest with your kids does not mean Telling Them Everything That Is Wrong With Them.

271. Don't call your child by his family nickname in front of his friends (unless he says it's okay).

272. Be on the lookout for hidden agendas that can affect your parenting: jealousy, anxiety over aging, conflict with your spouse, echoes from your own childhood.

273. Forget about yesterday. Today is a new opportunity for building a better relationship with your child.

274. Instead of asking every day the same old "How was school?" ask: "Did you see anything unfair happen at school today?" "What did you daydream about in social studies?" "What was the strangest/funniest/most useless thing you learned today?"

275. When your child speaks, give her your full attention. Put down the paper, mute the TV, stop what you're working on.

✷

276. If you want your children to confide in you, show them that it is safe to do so.

✷

277. Have a weekly family chore time when you turn the music up loud and spend thirty minutes doing your tasks. Then celebrate with pizza and ice cream (low fat, of course!).

✸

278. Remember that good parenting is not a set of rules. It is a set of attitudes.

✸

279. Allow your child her right to give. It is through giving that she develops self-esteem, and learns to trust and be trustworthy.

✹

280. The best way to get a child to clam up is to correct everything he says.

✹

281. Keep in mind that a messy room may be a sign that your child is highly creative. (Then again, it may just mean he's a slob.)

✹

282. Let your child express his anger. Otherwise it will stay with him.

✹

283. Take your child to work.

✹

284. Respond to your child's wrongdoing by focusing on how she can do better in the future rather than how she can be made to suffer for the past.

285. Don't contaminate praise with criticism.

PRAISE	CRITICISM
"What a great report card!"	"You see what you can do when you apply yourself."
"Don't you look nice!"	"I didn't recognize you."

Polluted praise sounds as if it's motivated by the expectation of bad behavior. What your child hears is "How wonderful that you're not your usual lazy, sloppy self."

✸

286. Remember that the way children learn to make good decisions is by making bad decisions.

✸

287. Don't confuse what you needed as a child with what your child needs from you now.

✸

288. Don't finish your child's sentences for her.

✸

289. If you're busy and can't respond to your child's need, commit yourself to a precise time when you can.

❋

290. Don't feel you have to "make better" whatever it is
     your child brings to you. Often, listening is enough.

❋

291. Never, ever, bribe your children. But do give treats just
     because you love them.

❋

292. Thank your kids for the little everyday things they do that contribute to the household.

✹

293. Give your child a valentine on August 14th.

✹

294. Don't entrap your child into a lie. If you saw her at the movies when she said she'd be at the library, tell her, and take it from there.

✵

295. Get down to your child's eye level when you speak. (How would you like to explain yourself to someone 18 feet tall!)

✵

296. Give your child unconditional love. This allows her to take risks without feeling you will love her the less if she fails.

297. How you think of your children is how they will come to think of themselves.

298. The time you spend with your child says: "I enjoy your company."

299. It is not your child's job to fulfill you.

300. Don't preach. Just practice.

�֍

301. Hitting a child is not discipline. It is violence.

✖

302. It is just as damaging to do too much for your child as it is to do not enough.

✳

303. Remember that conflict represents, not only disagreement, but caring.

✳

304. If your child is having trouble in school, it doesn't mean he's a problem child. He may just be going to a problem school.

✵

305. Your child cannot make you angry. If you feel anger, that is a choice you make.

✵

306. Make a list of everything you like and admire about your child.

✵

307. When things go wrong, the first thing to try is laughter.

308. Don't miss out on what your child is today by focusing on what you want him to become tomorrow.

309. Think of your actions in two ways:

> 1) how they affect your child, and
> 2) what they teach your child.

> A slap not only hurts a child, it teaches him that violence between loved ones is acceptable.

310. Involve your children in establishing family rules, rituals, and procedures.

311. When conflicts arise, don't yell, attack, shame, withdraw, sulk, deny, threaten, manipulate, frighten, or play doormat. Instead, ask your child: "Would you be willing to talk about this until we can find a solution that will work for both of us?"

312. To solve a problem:

1. Define it
2. Brainstorm solutions
3. Choose one
4. Act on it
5. Monitor progress and fine-tune as needed

313. Don't shield your child from pain. You may prevent him from growing.

✸

314. Remember that discipline based on fear is doomed to
fail the day your child ceases to be afraid of you.

✸

315. If your teenager asks that you not hug or kiss him in
front of his friends, respect his request. If he asks that
you do the same in private, respect his request but
protest vociferously.

✵

316. Teach your children to do their own laundry.

✵

317. Most parental fears come, not from reality, but from imagination.

318. When little sparks trigger big arguments, look beneath the surface for the real issue. Ask yourself (and your child): "What's really going on here?"

☀

319. Consult a therapist if your family relationships need some help.

☀

320. It's not called "blind rage" for nothing. If you're so angry you're seeing red, disengage. Tell your child, "I need to calm down before I can discuss this."

321. Remember that worry is the most useless mental activity ever invented.

322. Never lecture or get into discipline issues over dinner. Dinner is for civilized conversation about school, work, current events, politics, philosophy, religion, music, art, sports, travel, and Barney.

323. Take a class together with your child.

324. Always have an event on the calendar to which you and your child are looking forward.

325. Go through the house with your kids and identify and correct safety hazards.

326. Treat your child's ideas and feelings as you would gifts; even if they are not to your taste, express appreciation that they were given.

327. Be consistent without being inflexible.

328. Before you decide that your child can't be trusted, find out *why* she did what she did. Irresponsible actions sometimes result from laudable motives.

329. Don't mistake dawdling for disobedience. A child's sense of time is different from an adult's.

330. Remember what you were like at that age.

✳

331. Don't worry about what the neighbors will think.

✳

332. Help your child to divide her dreams into manageable steps.

✷

333. Make music together.

✷

334. Ask your child to tell you ten things she likes about herself. Then tell her ten things *you* like about her.

✷

335. Go for after-dinner walks with your children.

336. Create a video family album with your kids. Interview grandparents, aunts, uncles, cousins, family friends.

337. Don't turn requests for help into lecture opportunities.

✶

338. Keep an agenda posted where family members can jot down issues to discuss at family meetings.

✶

339. Treat your child with the same courtesy you would a stranger.

340. Try to establish reasonable guidelines with your teen-ager about drinking. Outright prohibitions rarely work and do nothing to develop responsibility. Most important is that your child know that he can count on you for a recrimination-free ride home, or cab fare, if he (or anyone driving) has had something to drink. (You can get reimbursed and discuss the event the next day.) It is better to have an honest drinker than a dead liar.

341. Remember that what's important to you and what's important to your child are two different universes. Don't belittle the things and people your child values. (This just *proves* your child is right when she says, "You don't understand.")

�֍

342. Play "This Little Piggy" with your teenager.

✷

343. Challenge your child to a game at his favorite video arcade. Bring a pocketful of quarters.

344. Be honest about your own youthful foibles when your children ask. (They can tell if you're lying, anyway.)

345. Give every family member the right to call a "time-out" when things get heated during a family discussion. The person who calls the time-out has to specify when he'll be ready to deal with the problem again—as long as it's sometime that day so everyone doesn't go to bed angry.

346. Make your child's friends welcome at your house.

347. Resist the temptation to apply facile philosophic Band-Aids to your child's disappointments.

�֎

348. From the beginning, be willing to talk with your child about anything. If you don't know the answer to a question, go to the library together and look it up. Later in life, when your child has questions about sex and other "big issues," she won't be embarrassed to come to you.

✸

349. Expect more of your children than they expect of themselves—neither party will be disappointed.

✸

350. Tell your children that there probably is a God, even if you're not sure yourself: you do it with Santa Claus, the Easter Bunny, and the Tooth Fairy. God's a much better bet.

✾

351. Instead of rushing your child, allow more time to get where you're going.

✾

352. Don't sweat the little stuff.

✾

353. Strive to be fair even though most things aren't.

✳

354. Never let your child divide you from your spouse. (If there is an issue where you and your spouse disagree, try to work it out in private. If you can't resolve it, tell your child that you disagree, but you are going to take *this* stand.)

✳

355. Notice and thank your child if she does something without being asked.

356. Read some of the books your child brings home for English. Talk about them.

357. Let your kids have pets. It teaches responsibility and friendship.

358. Never be your child's safety net unless the consequences of a "fall" are irreversible.

359. Don't tolerate whining. Say: "That's a whining voice. I don't hear whining voices. Use your regular voice." A grown-up voice is more likely to produce grown-up thoughts.

360. Teach your children to stand up whenever an adult enters the room. ????

✸

361. Teach your children to shake hands with people to whom they are introduced and to say, "It's nice to meet you."

✸

362. Teach your children to look at grown-ups' eyes when they talk to them.

✸

363. The praise your children will receive for their good manners will be a constant source of pride to them (and to you!).

✸

364. Stand behind your child no matter what. If he did something wrong he needs your support more than ever as he straightens out the mess.

365. Watch your child sleep.